with pull-out answer section

QUESTIONS in STANDARD GRADE SCIENCE

MORAG BARNES AND GRAEME BURT

Published by Leckie & Leckie
8 Whitehill Terrace
St Andrews KY16 8RN
Tel. 01334 475656
Fax. 01334 477392
E-mail: s.leckie@leckie-and-leckie.co.uk
Web site: www.leckie-and-leckie.co.uk

Illustrations by Suzanne Greig

Edited by Colin Biernat

Thanks also to Alison Irving, Susanna Kirk, Fiona McNee, Bruce Ryan and Hamish Sanderson

ISBN 1-898890-75-7

Copyright © 1997 Morag Barnes and Graeme Burt

All rights reserved. No part of this publication may be stored in a retrieval system, or transmitted in any form or by any means, electronic, mechanical, photocopying, recording or otherwise, without the prior permission in writing from Leckie & Leckie (Publishers).

A CIP Catalogue record for this book is available from the British Library.

Leckie & Leckie

Contents

Introduction		3
1. Healthy and Safe Living	Lungs and breathing	5
	Heart and blood supply	7
	Fit for life	9
2. An Introduction to Materials	Classification	13
	Uses and properties	15
	Improving materials	17
	Strength and shape of structures	18
	Flammability	19
	Protection of materials	20
	Miscellaneous materials questions	21
3. Energy and its Uses	Energy in the home	22
	Electrical safety	24
	Fossil fuels	25
	Nuclear energy	29
	Renewable energy	30
4. A Study of Environments	Food chains and food webs	31
	Interdependence and populations	34
	Production and recycling of household waste	36
	Pollution	37
	Human needs and conservation	40

Introduction

The questions in this book will help you to prepare for your Standard Grade Science exam.

- The topics which make up the course are:
  1. Healthy and Safe Living
  2. An Introduction to Materials
  3. Energy and its Uses
  4. A Study of Environments.

  The questions in this book are set out in this order.

- Answers are provided in the centre section. These pages are removable.

- To help you in your revision, the answer section shows you which questions are Foundation level, which are General level and which are Credit level using the following system:

  > Answers to Foundation level questions are printed on a white background (like this).
  > Answers to General level questions are printed on a hatched background (like this).
  > Answers to Credit level questions are printed on a shaded background (like this).

  You should attempt all the questions. Check with your teacher, however, about which levels you are sitting in the exam.

- Spend time revising each topic and then try the questions on that topic. To help you with your revision, we recommend that you obtain a copy of Leckie & Leckie's other Standard Grade Science book, *Standard Grade Science Revision Notes*, from your school or bookshop.

  At the foot of every page of questions you will find a page reference to Leckie & Leckie's *Standard Grade Science Revision Notes*. Look up these pages for help with answering the questions.

- Use a jotter or paper for your answers. To answer some questions you will need graph paper, a calculator and a ruler.

- Both Knowledge and Understanding and Problem Solving questions are included for each topic.

  - Knowledge and Understanding questions test how much you have learned and remembered. To do well, you need to learn facts. This takes time and effort.

  - Problem Solving questions are designed to test skills which you have developed in the course.

    - For Foundation level you must be able to:
      - calculate a percentage
      - do calculations (adding, subtracting, multiplying or dividing)
      - draw a conclusion
      - complete a table
      - complete a graph
      - identify a fair experiment.

    - For General level you must also be able to:
      - draw a graph
      - predict results
      - construct a food web
      - construct a key
      - calculate an average
      - describe how to set up a fair experiment.

    - For Credit level you must also be able to:
      - explain experiment results
      - use a formula to do a calculation
      - draw a line graph with two lines
      - comment on improvements to an experiment
      - do calculations involving multiplication and addition, or multiplication and subtraction.

Good luck with your exam.

1. Healthy and Safe Living

Lungs and breathing

1. The diagram below shows parts of the body. What labels should be added to the three arrows in the diagram?

   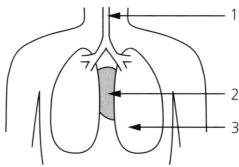

2. You breathe to get air into and out of your lungs.
   (a) The ribs are moved by muscles between the ribs.
       In what direction do the ribs move when you breathe in?
   (b) (i) Another muscular structure is involved in the movements of breathing.
           Name this structure.
       (ii) What happens to this structure when you breathe out?

3. Andy's breathing rate was measured during different activities.
   The results are shown in the table below.

Activity	sleeping	watching TV	walking	walking upstairs	playing football
Average breathing rate (breaths per minute)	10	12	16	24	32

   (a) Andy walks for 20 minutes.
       How many breaths will he take in this time?
   (b) What is the increase in breathing rate between walking and playing football?
   (c) What conclusion can you draw from these results about how active you are and how this affects your breathing rate?
   (d) Predict Andy's breathing rate as he finishes a 200 m race.

4. The diagram below represents an air sac in the lungs.

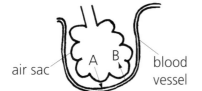

Gases pass into and out of the blood through air sacs.

(a) What gases are represented by the letters A and B in the diagram?

(b) Name the substance in the blood which joins to oxygen.

5. Describe how mucus and cilia (tiny hairs) in the windpipe and air passages help to keep the lungs clean.

6. Smoking cigarettes can damage your health.
   Copy and complete the table to show this.

Substance in tobacco smoke	Effect on body	Linked disease
tar		
	stops cilia working	bronchitis
	stops blood from carrying oxygen	

7. Harmful substances can enter the body through the lungs.

Coal miners may breathe in coal dust at their work, which may lead to lung disease.
Give one other example of how a harmful substance may be breathed in.

8. Approximately 120 000 people in the UK develop lung cancer every year.
   20% of these cases are suitable for surgical treatment.
   How many lung cancer patients can receive surgical treatment in one year?

Heart and blood supply

9. What is the function of the heart?

10. The diagram on the right shows the structure of the heart.

    (a) Name the parts labelled 1 and 4 in the diagram.

    (b) The structures labelled 5, 6 and 7 all have the same function.
        (i) What name is given to these structures?
        (ii) What is the function of these structures?

    (c) Which number labels the part of the heart which pumps blood to the lungs?

    (d) What are the walls of the heart made of?

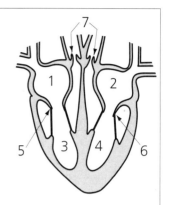

11. There are three main types of blood vessels which carry blood round the body.

    (a) Copy and complete the table.

Type of blood vessel	Blood pressure	Direction of blood flow	Diagram
	high		
	low	through body organs	
		back to the heart	

    (b)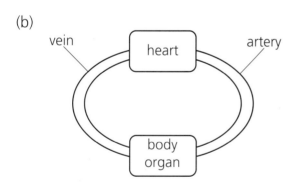

    Copy the diagram and add arrows to show the direction of blood flow in the artery and vein.

12. Alastair took his own pulse rate. It was 92 beats per minute.

     What was his heart rate?

13. Average heart rate is 70 beats per minute.
    During very vigorous exercise this can rise to 210 beats per minute.
    (a) Why does the heart rate increase during exercise?
    (b) What is the percentage increase in the heart rates given above?
    (c) Which part of the heart controls the rate of beating?

14. The heart rates of two people, Alex and Mike, were measured. The rates were taken at rest, then during and then after exercise. They took the same exercise.

    The results were graphed.

    (a) Who is fitter, Alex or Mike? Explain your answer.
    (b) If exercise continues for a long time, two waste products build up in the body. Name these waste products.
    (c) What term is used to describe the time between the end of exercise and the heart rate returning to normal?

    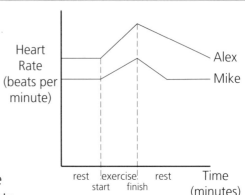

15. (a) State the function of each of the following parts of the blood:
    (i) red blood cells
    (ii) plasma
    (iii) platelets.
    (b) Describe two ways by which white blood cells help to defend the body against germs and disease.

16. The body's defence system can be prepared in advance to fight off some diseases.
    In childhood, we can be _____ against diseases such as mumps, measles and rubella.
    What is the missing word in the sentence above?

17. Heart disease can occur when the heart's own blood vessels stop working properly.
    List four factors which increase the risk of developing heart disease.

Fit for life

18. (a) What is human normal body temperature?

    (b) Copy and complete the sentences by selecting the correct words from the wordbank.

    Human body temperature is normally _____ than the surroundings.
    If body temperature starts to rise, we _____ to keep cool.
    If body temperature starts to fall, we _____ to warm up again.
    If body temperature falls dangerously low, the person is suffering from _____.

Wordbank	hyperthermia, lower, sweat, salivate, shiver, higher, hypothermia

    (c) Our bodies constantly gain more heat energy to replace heat lost from the skin to the air. How is this energy supplied to the body?

19. A class set up an experiment to measure heat loss from the human body in different conditions.

    The pupils used plastic bottles as model bodies and filled them with water at 40°C. All the bottles were filled at the same time and placed in different conditions for 10 minutes. The classroom temperature was 20°C.
    One group left bottle 1 untouched in the classroom. After 10 minutes its temperature was 34°C.
    The second group put bottle 2 in the fridge. It went down to 24°C.
    The third group covered bottle 3 with wet cloth and after 10 minutes, the water inside measured 30°C.
    The fourth group covered their bottle with dry cloth. It went down to 36°C.
    The fifth bottle was set up so that cold air from a hairdryer blew over it (windy conditions). Its water temperature went down to 28°C.

    (a) Calculate the temperature drop in each of the five conditions.

    (b) Present the above results, showing the drops in temperature in a table with suitable headings.

    (c) Predict:
      (i) the temperature of the first bottle if left in the classroom for 2 hours
      (ii) the temperature of water in a bottle set up in the same way as in the experiment but covered in wet cloth and blown with cold air from a hairdryer.

    (d) The groups put their results together and drew conclusions.
      (i) Which two bottles would be compared to draw the conclusion: 'Clothes help keep your body warm'?
      (ii) Which two bottles would be compared to draw the conclusion: 'Your body will lose more heat in cold air than in warm air'?

    (e) To make the experiment reliable, it should have been repeated and average results calculated. What should have been done to make sure the experiment was fair (valid)?

20. In the UK, many deaths from cancers can be related to known factors.

Factor	Average number of cancer deaths per year
tobacco	210 000
alcohol	30 000
diet	210 000
infection	24 000
job	30 000

Present the above information as a bar graph, using graph paper.

21. A varied diet will help keep you healthy.
Every day you should eat bread or pasta, milk products and meat or meat alternatives.
What other group of food should you eat to keep healthy?

22. Scottish people have a reputation for not eating a healthy varied diet. Name a health problem that could be caused by eating too much fat and sugar.

23. If your food contains more energy than you need, the extra energy will be stored as fat.
What word can be used to describe someone who is excessively fat?

24. The table below shows ideal weights for females at age 20–25.
The ideal weights for males are 2 kg heavier at each height.

Height (m)	Ideal Female Weight (kg)
1·50	48
1·55	50
1·60	52
1·65	55
1·70	59

(a) Predict the ideal weight for a female who is 1·45 m tall.
(b) Predict the ideal weight for a male who is 1·58 m tall.

25. A girl buys a sandwich for lunch.
    She reads the information on the pack.

Ingredients	Energy per 100 g (kJ)
bread	977
vegetable spread	2260
cheese	1700

    The sandwich contains two slices (100 g each) of bread, 10 g of vegetable spread and 20 g of cheese.
    How much energy will she get from the sandwich?

26. Linda's mother is worried about her. She has become very thin. She tries to avoid eating with the family and is obsessed with reading about diets.
    What could be wrong with Linda?

27. A boy ate 200 g of chicken. 15% of the chicken was fat.
    How much fat did he eat?

28. Many people enjoy a social life which involves drinking alcohol.
    (a) (i) Name one illness which could be caused by drinking too much alcohol too often.
        (ii) Give one way the alcohol will affect the behaviour of a person who drinks too much.
    (b) One bottle of wine contains enough for six glasses.
        How many units of alcohol are in one bottle of wine?
    (c) Ewan drank two pints of beer and Kirsty drank three glasses of wine. How many units of alcohol had Ewan and Kirsty drunk altogether?

29. The graph below shows a man's blood alcohol content over a period of time.

    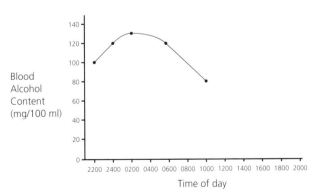

    (a) What is the highest blood alcohol level recorded?
    (b) What was the increase in blood alcohol in the first two hours?
    (c) The legal blood alcohol limit for driving is 80 mg/100 ml. At what time would the man be fit to drive?
    (d) Predict the time at which his blood alcohol content will reach 0 mg/100 ml.

30. Here is part of an index from a cookbook.

Aduki beans 480	Aniseed 488
Almonds	Apples 299–300
biscuits 410	cake 375
cookies 408	jam 460
caramels 414	pie 344
Anchovies 170	Apricots 301
Angel cake 380	

Which two pages would you look up to find information about cakes?

31. (a) There are three different aspects to fitness, known as 'the three Ss'. Name all three.

(b) Which of the three aspects will be improved by:
 (i) regular long distance running
 (ii) regular bending and twisting exercises?

(c) Name an exercise which will improve all three aspects of fitness.

2. An Introduction to Materials

Classification

32. What does the term 'classification' mean?

33. (a) Copy and complete the table below using the list of substances provided.

Solids	Liquids	Gases

All these substances are at room temperature:

iron   methane   air   mercury   carbon dioxide
petrol   glass   cork   vinegar   steel
lemonade   oxygen   water   perspex   nitrogen
polythene   rubber   hydrogen   wood   hydrochloric acid

(b) Fiona has classified some materials. What should the two headings be?

copper	rubber
steel	polystyrene
brass	wood
iron	clay
aluminium	nylon

34. (a) You have to classify 'aluminium'. From the options listed below choose the group (or groups) into which aluminium would fit.

A. Metals   B. Non-metals   C. Solids   D. Liquids   E. Gases

(b) You also have to classify 'polystyrene'. Choose the group (or groups) from the options listed below into which polystyrene would fit.

A. Natural materials   B. Man-made materials   C. Metals   D. Non-metals

35. Moira was given the task of classifying a large box of substances. Later, she produced a bar chart showing the results of her work:

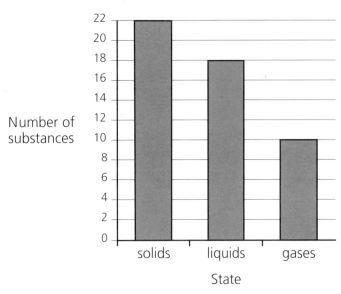

(a) What was the total number of substances classified by Moira?

(b) What percentage of the substances classified were liquids?

(c) How many of the substances classified could be put into a completely new group called 'non-solids'?

36. The list below shows different clothing materials.

   wool   silk
   nylon   lycra
   polyester cotton
   rayon   terylene

   Construct a table with **two** suitable headings to classify these materials.

37. Some materials can be used for many different purposes:
   e.g. rubber can be used for • tyres
                                 • shoe soles
                                 • toys
   For each of the materials below give three different uses:

   (a) steel (b) wood (c) glass (d) nylon (e) copper

38. Rita Rich is having new double-glazed windows made and fitted in her doll's house. The toy maker would like to make the window frames exactly like those fitted in 'real' houses. Name three materials he could use to make the frames.

Uses and properties

39.

1 steel	2 wood	3 glass
4 cardboard	5 polystyrene	6 copper

Use this table of materials when answering questions (a) to (e) below:

(a) Which **three** boxes contain materials used to make frying pan bases?

(b) Which **two** boxes contain materials most likely to be used for packaging around new television sets?

(c) Which **two** boxes contain materials most likely to be used to make kitchen spoons?

(d) Which **one** box contains the material most likely to be used for electrical wiring?

(e) Which **one** box contains the material most likely to be used to make a craft knife blade?

40. You have to choose the material to use for the handle of a frying pan. Which one of the properties listed below is most important?

   A. resistance to corrosion
   B. flexibility
   C. thermal conductivity
   D. wear resistance

41. You are designing a fishing rod. You have to choose a material to make it from. Which one of the properties listed below is most important?

   A. wear resistance
   B. flexibility
   C. thermal conductivity
   D. resistance to corrosion

42. You have to choose a material for the blade of a saw. Which one of the properties listed below is the most important?

   A. hardness
   B. heat resistance
   C. resistance to corrosion
   D. thermal conductivity

43. Lycra is a material that is now widely used in clothes design.
    (a) What is the main advantage that lycra has over other materials?
    (b) Give three examples of the types of clothes for which lycra is particularly suitable.

44. Match each of the properties listed below (1–6) to its correct definition (A–F).

Property
1. thermal conductivity
2. flexibility
3. flammability
4. electrical conductivity
5. strength
6. elasticity

Definition
A. ability to catch fire
B. ability to conduct electricity
C. ability to stretch
D. ability to conduct heat
E. ability to bend without damage
F. ability to withstand great force without bending or breaking

45. Sarah tested the strengths of four different threads. She did this by hanging weights from each thread – she added more and more weights until the thread snapped. She repeated this four more times with each thread. Sarah's results are shown below.

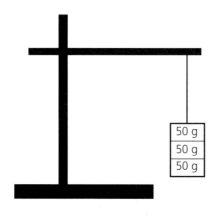

Test	Breaking weights of threads (g)			
	Thread A	Thread B	Thread C	Thread D
1	550	800	750	900
2	600	600	700	700
3	650	700	700	600
4	650	750	700	500
5	550	650	700	900

(a) Why did Sarah repeat the experiment to give five results for each thread?

(b) Calculate the average breaking weights for each thread.

(c) From Sarah's results, which thread is the strongest?

(d) (i) Which thread would be the most reliable if it had to withstand a weight of 680 g?
    (ii) Explain your choice.

(e) Which two things (about the threads) must be kept constant to ensure a fair comparison?

Improving materials

46. What is the term used to describe a mixture of two or more metals?

47. Which two metals are mixed to produce brass?

48. Which three metals are mixed to produce solder?

49. The graph below shows how the strength of steel changes as the carbon content of the steel increases.

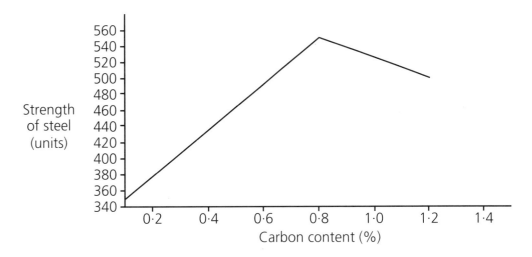

(a) What is the carbon content of the strongest steel?

(b) Predict the strength of steel with a 1·4% carbon content.

50. Stainless steel has a high chromium content. What is the major advantage of stainless steel over 'normal' steel (i.e. steel with a much lower chromium content)?

51. Natural fibres (such as cotton and wool) are often more comfortable to wear than man-made fibres. Many clothes are made by mixing natural and man-made fibres. What is one advantage of mixing cotton and polyester, instead of using pure cotton?

52. Concrete is a mixture of which four materials? Choose one of the options listed below.

    A. sand, cement, clay and water   C. sand, clay, stones and water

    B. sand, cement, stones and water   D. cement, clay, stones and water

53. The process of tempering steel is done by heating the steel to around 900°C, quickly cooling it in water and then warming it up again to about 300°C. How does tempered steel differ from other forms of steel?

54. What is the name given to the alloy that is a mixture of lead and tin?

55. Why would brass screws sometimes be better than steel screws?

Strength and shape of structures

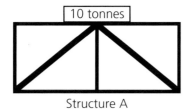
Structure A

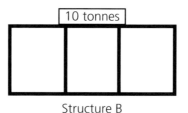
Structure B

56. (a) Which of these structures is stronger?

    (b) Explain your answer.

57. (a) Draw the shape of a corrugated metal sheet.

    (b) Explain why corrugations are used.

    (c) Give an example of corrugation that you might see being carried home from your local supermarket.

58. Name three shapes of girder that are much stronger than a solid girder of exactly the same weight.

Flammability

59. What does flammable mean?

60. What is a fuel?

61. Which gas is required for something to burn?

62. William tested three flameproofing chemicals. He treated three pieces of cotton with the three chemicals and left a fourth piece of cotton untreated. He then took one of the pieces of cotton and held it over a bunsen burner flame. He repeated this with the other three pieces of cotton, each time recording how long it took for the piece of cotton to be set alight.

    William's results are shown below.

Sample	Time taken to catch fire (s)
cotton treated with chemical A	11
cotton treated with chemical B	8
cotton treated with chemical C	9
cotton untreated	3

    WARNING!

    This experiment should only be attempted in a controlled, supervised classroom.

    (a) What should William have done to make his results more reliable?
    (b) Do William's results suggest that flameproofing works?
    (c) William's experiment was fair. Suggest three things that William must have kept constant.

63. Which poisonous gas is given off when polyurethane foam burns?

64. Which poisonous gas is given off when P.V.C. (polyvinyl chloride) burns?

Protection of materials

65. What is the name given to the type of polystyrene used to protect electrical equipment? (It is usually found tightly packed around the equipment in the box when new.)
   Choose one of the options below.
   A. extended polystyrene
   B. exploded polystyrene
   C. expounded polystyrene
   D. expanded polystyrene

66. (a) (i) What is a woodworm attack?
       (ii) How can it be treated?
   (b) (i) What is wet rot?
       (ii) How can it be prevented?
   (c) (i) What is dry rot?
       (ii) How can it be prevented?

67. What word is defined in a dictionary as:

    'the slow wearing away of solids, especially metals, by chemical attack'?

68. What two substances must be present for iron to rust?
    Choose one of the options below.
    A. carbon dioxide and water
    B. oxygen and water
    C. nitrogen and water
    D. nitrogen and oxygen
    E. air and nitrogen

69. What is the chemical name for rust?

70. Explain how painting iron or steel prevents rusting.

71. Which metal is used to galvanise steel? Choose one from the options below.
    A. zinc   B. copper   C. lead   D. tin

72. What is electroplating?

73. Which metal is protected by anodising? Choose one from the options below.
    A. iron   B. aluminium   C. steel   D. copper

Answers to Leckie & Leckie's *Questions in Standard Grade Science*

Answers to Foundation level questions are printed on a white background (like this).
Answers to General level questions are printed on a hatched background (like this).
Answers to Credit level questions are printed on a shaded background (like this).

1. Healthy and Safe Living

Lungs and breathing

1. 1 = windpipe, 2 = heart, 3 = lung

2. (a) The ribs move out and up when you breathe in.
   (b) (i) diaphragm
       (ii) It moves up.

3. (a) 16 breaths per minute × 20 minutes = 320 breaths.
   (b) playing football = 32, walking = 16.
       therefore increase = 32 − 16
                         = 16 breaths per minute.
   (c) The more active you are, the faster your breathing rate.
   (d) Running is very active, so answers of 32 breaths per minute or more are accepted.

4. (a) A = oxygen, B = carbon dioxide.
   (b) haemoglobin

5. • Mucus traps dust and germs.
   • Cilia move the mucus with dust and germs up and out of the lungs.

6.
Substances in tobacco smoke	Effect on body	Linked disease
tar	sticks to/builds up in air passages	lung cancer
nicotine	stops cilia working	bronchitis
carbon monoxide	stops blood from carrying oxygen	heart disease

7. You can breathe in smoke or waste gases from factories or houses, traffic exhaust fumes or solvents from glue.

8. 20% of 120 000 means 20% × 120 000
   or $\frac{20}{100} \times 120\,000 = 24\,000$

Heart and blood supply

9. The heart pumps blood round the body.

10. (a) 1 = right atrium/auricle
        4 = left ventricle
    (b) (i) valves
        (ii) to stop blood flowing in the wrong direction/prevent backflow of blood
    (c) 3
    (d) muscle

11. (a)
Type of blood vessel	Blood pressure	Direction of blood flow	Diagram
artery	high	away from the heart	
capillary	low	through body organs	
vein	low	back to the heart	

   (b) vein — heart — artery — body organ

12. Pulse rate = heart rate,
    therefore heart rate = 92 beats per minute.

13. (a) The heart rate increases to pump more blood to the muscles. More blood brings more oxygen to burn food to release more energy.
        The extra blood also takes away the carbon dioxide waste produced when extra food is burnt in the body.
    (b) First calculate the increase:
        210 − 70 = 140
        Now calculate the percentage increase:
        $\frac{\text{increase}}{\text{original}} = \frac{140}{70} \times 100 = 200\%$
    (c) pacemaker

Answers page 1

14. (a)	Mike is fitter. *Any one from:* his heart rate is lower at rest, his heart rate does not increase as much during exercise and his heart rate returns to normal more quickly.	15. (b)	White cells produce antibodies. White cells engulf ('eat') germs.
(b)	carbon dioxide and lactic acid	16.	In childhood, we can be *immunised* against diseases such as mumps, measles and rubella.
(c)	recovery time	17.	*Any four from:* · smoking · being overweight · bad diet · lack of exercise · worry or stress · inherited factors (history of heart disease in the family).
15. (a)	(i) Red blood cells carry oxygen. (ii) Plasma carries food, heat and water round the body. (iii) Platelets clot the blood/form clots to stop bleeding.		

Fit for life

18. (a)	37°C	20.	(bar chart: Average number of cancer deaths per year (thousands) vs Factor — tobacco ~200, alcohol ~30, diet ~200, infection ~20, job ~30)
(b)	Human body temperature is normally *higher* than the surroundings. If body temperature starts to rise, we *sweat* to keep cool. If body temperature starts to fall, we *shiver* to warm up again. If body temperature falls dangerously low, the person is suffering from *hypothermia*.	21.	fruit and vegetables
		22.	*Any one from:* · heart disease · obesity · high blood pressure
(c)	by burning food in the body	23.	obese
19. (a)	Temperature drops: 1 = 6°C, 2 = 16°C, 3 = 10°C, 4 = 4°C, 5 = 12°C	24. (a)	46 kg (Any figure between and including 45 kg and 47 kg would be accepted.)
(b)	A number of headings would be accepted as long as conditions and temperatures are displayed. Units must be included with the headings for temperature.	(b)	Any figure between and including 52 kg and 54 kg accepted.
e.g.	(table below)	25.	2520 kJ. i.e. 2 × 100 g slices of bread = 2 × 977 kJ = 1954 kJ 10 g veg. spread = 2260 ÷ $\frac{100}{10}$ = 2260 ÷ 10 = 226 kJ 20 g cheese = 1700 ÷ $\frac{100}{20}$ = 1700 ÷ 5 = 340 kJ Total = 2520 kJ

Bottle condition	Start temp. (°C)	Finish temp. (°C)	Temperature drop (°C)
in classroom	40	34	6
in fridge	40	24	16
wet cloth cover	40	30	10
dry cloth cover	40	36	4
'wind' blowing	40	28	12

(c)	(i) 20°C (It would fall to room temperature.) (ii) Any temperature less than 28°C	26.	She could be suffering from anorexia nervosa.
		27.	15% of 200 g means 15% × 200 g = $\frac{15}{100}$ × 200 g = 30 g of fat
(d)	(i) 1 and 4 (ii) 1 and 2		
(e)	All bottles should: be same size, be same type, have same volume of water, have same thermometer, have thermometer held at the same depth for readings.	28. (a)	(i) *Any one from:* · stomach ulcer · cirrhosis of the liver · heart disease · brain damage
			(ii) *Any one from:* · feel reckless · fall over · slur speech · pick fights · lack judgement
		(b)	6 units (1 glass of wine = 1 unit of alcohol)

28. (c) Ewan had 2 pints of beer = 4 units of alcohol. Kirsty had 3 glasses of wine = 3 units of alcohol. 4 + 3 = 7 units altogether	29. (d) Any time between 1800 and 2000 accepted
	30. pages 380 and 375
29. (a) 130 mg/100 ml	31. (a) strength, suppleness, stamina
(b) 20 mg/100 ml	(b) (i) stamina (ii) suppleness
(c) at 1000	(c) swimming (or another named all-round exercise)

2. An Introduction to Materials

Classification

32. Dividing into groups

33. (a)

Solids	Liquids	Gases
iron	petrol	methane
polythene	lemonade	oxygen
glass	water	air
rubber	mercury	hydrogen
cork	vinegar	carbon dioxide
perspex	hydrochloric acid	nitrogen
wood		
steel		

(b)

Metals	Non-metals

34. (a) A and C
(b) B and D

35. (a) 22 + 18 + 10 = 50

35. (b) $\dfrac{18}{50} \times \dfrac{100}{1} = 36\%$

(c) 28 (18 liquids and 10 gases)

36.

Natural	Man-made
wool	nylon
silk	polyester
cotton	rayon
	lycra
	terylene

37. In each answer other sensible uses are acceptable.
(a) bridges, cutlery, tools
(b) desks, houses, furniture
(c) windows, spectacles, bottles
(d) rope, clothes, thread
(e) pipes, coins, wiring

38. aluminium, PVC, wood

Uses and properties

39. (a) 1, 3, 6   (d) 6
(b) 4, 5   (e) 1
(c) 1, 2

40. C
41. B
42. A
43. (a) Lycra is stretchy (has good elasticity).
(b) It is suitable for swimsuits, cycle shorts, leotards and other sportswear.

44. 1 – D   4 – B
2 – E   5 – F
3 – A   6 – C

45. (a) To get averages – which are more reliable results.
(b) Thread A – 600 g
Thread B – 700 g
Thread C – 710 g
Thread D – 720 g
(c) Thread D
(d) (i) Thread C
(ii) <u>All</u> results using thread C were above 680 g.
(e) Length and thickness must be kept constant.

Improving materials

46. alloy	51. The mixture is more hard-wearing than pure cotton.
47. copper and zinc	52. B
48. copper, zinc and tin	53. Tempered steel is springier (more flexible) than normal steel.
49. (a) 0·8% (b) 460 to 480 units	54. pewter
50. Stainless steel does not rust.	55. Brass does not rust.

Strength and shape of structures

56. (a) A (b) Triangles are stronger shapes than rectangles. 57. (a)	57. (b) Corrugations are used to make the sheets stronger. (c) An example is the walls of a cardboard box.
	58. *Any three from:* tube, H-shape, T-shape, box

Flammability

59. 'Flammable' means able to catch fire easily.	62. (c) *Any three from:* • same area of cloth • same thickness of cloth • same height above flame • same volume of chemical added
60. A fuel is a material which burns.	
61. oxygen	
62. (a) He should have repeated each test several times to get averages. (b) Yes (the untreated cloth caught fire quicker than any of the treated cloths).	63. hydrogen cyanide
	64. hydrogen chloride

Protection of materials

65. D	68. B
66. (a) (i) an attack by insect larvae that eat wood (ii) chemical spray (b) (i) wood being rotted by water (ii) by using wood preservative (c) (i) a fungus affecting wood (ii) by using wood preservative	69. iron oxide
	70. Painting stops oxygen and water reaching the metal.
	71. A
	72. coating one metal with another using electricity
	73. B
67. corrosion	

Miscellaneous materials questions

74. (a) 50% (b) 6 kg (c) 12 kg	76. prevents red blood cells from carrying oxygen around body
75. *Any three e.g.* pyjamas, curtains, armchairs, sofas	77. (a) Jill (b) Tubes are very strong (from end to end) but less strong on their sides.

Answers page 4

3. Energy and its Uses

Energy in the home

78. 29613 − 26406 = 3207
    3207 × 8 = £256·56

79.

Appliance	Time of use (hours)	Energy used (kWh)	Cost per kWh	Total cost
100 W bulb	10	1·0	8 p	8 p
2·5 kW fire	4	10	8 p	80 p
1·0 kW iron	2	2	8 p	16 p
2 kW fan heater	6	12	8 p	96 p
200 W freezer	100	20	8 p	£1·60

80. (a) to keep a constant fixed temperature
    (b) *Any three from:* iron, oven, central heating, washing machine, fridge, freezer
    (c) When the heater is on, the temperature rises and the bimetallic strip bends, so electrical contact is broken and the heater goes off.
    When the heater is off, the temperature drops and the strip straightens, so contact is made and the heater goes on.
    When the heater is on, etc.

81. (a) (i) loft insulation
       (ii) *Any one from:* double glazing, draught-proofing, curtains
       (iii) carpets
       (iv) cavity wall insulation
       (v) draught excluders
    (b) convection

82. (a) walls
    (b) 10%
    (c) loft insulation because loss through the roof is much higher therefore potential savings (of energy and money) are greater.

Electrical safety

83.

Wire	Name	Colour
1	Neutral	blue
2	Earth	green/yellow
3	Live	brown

84. The Earth wire is a *safety* device. It is connected to the outer casing of *metal* appliances. If a *fault* occurs and the outer casing becomes *live*, the *earth* wire will carry a large *current* to ground and cause the *fuse* to melt. The appliance is now *off* and therefore *safe*.

85. (a) 13 amp (c) 13 amp (e) 13 amp
    (b) 3 amp   (d) 3 amp   (f) 13 amp

86. (a) = 10, (b) = 600, (c) = 1200, (d) = 3·4

87. C

88. The fuse is a safety device. It is a thin piece of wire designed to melt if the current is too high. This switches off the supply.

89. The Live wire carries the current. Therefore, when switch is off or the fuse is broken there is no current.

Fossil fuels

90. (a) Renewable energy sources will never run out.
    (b) Non-renewable energy sources will run out.

91. *Any three for each:*
    <u>Renewable</u> – wind, waves, solar, geothermal
    <u>Non-renewable</u> – coal, oil, gas, peat, nuclear

92. Plants died and fell into swamp. Over millions of years layer upon layer of rock pressed down on this material. This turned the material into coal.

93. Oil started as dead <u>animals and plants</u> <u>under the sea</u>. Coal started as <u>plants</u> on <u>land</u>.

94. a = gas, b = oil, c = water

95. (a) Seismic – small explosions – study shape of echoes from rocks.
    (b) Aerial – photographs taken from the air.
    (c) Geological – study local rock types and maps.

96. (a) 25%

96. (b) (i) 400 gigajoules
    (ii) 200 gigajoules
    (iii) 200 gigajoules

97. The crude oil extracted from the ground has to be refined, i.e. split into useful parts in a fractionating tower. The parts into which the oil is split are called fractions. This process depends upon the different parts having different boiling points. The temperature at the bottom of the tower is much higher and therefore substances with high boiling points are taken off there. Substances from the bottom of the tower are dark coloured whereas those substances from higher up the tower (with lower boiling points) are light coloured.

98. (a) (i) sulphur dioxide
    (ii) Acid rain kills trees and plants, kills fish and damages buildings.
    (b) (i) carbon dioxide
    (ii) Carbon dioxide raises the temperature of the planet and may change weather patterns.

99.

Product	Use	Extraction point
petrol	fuel for cars	B
bitumen (tar)	for road surfaces	D
naphtha	for making plastics	B
petroleum gases	fuel gases	A
diesel	fuel for lorries	C
paraffin	fuel for heating/ aviation fuel	B
wax	for making candles	D

100. Chemical energy → Heat energy → Movement (Kinetic) energy → Electrical energy.

101. Boiler, Turbine, Generator.

102. (a) 223
     (b) 101
     (c) Any two from: 185, 194, 205

103. 1 – B, 2 – A, 3 – C, 4 – C, 5 – C

Nuclear energy

104. (a)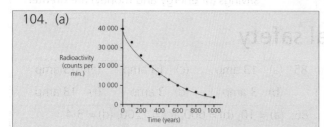

104. (b) any figure between 27 000 and 29 000
     (c) (i) 'Half-life' means the time for radioactivity to fall to half of its previous value.
         (ii) 300 years

105. C

Renewable energy

106. E = 5 × 4200 × (70 – 20) = 1 050 000 joules

107. (a)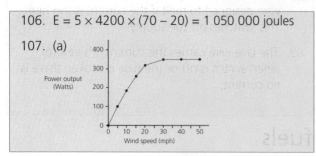

107. (b) Up to 30 mph, the greater the wind speed, the greater the power output.

The generator has an optimum (best) wind speed of about 30 mph – any further increase will not improve the power output.

108. geothermal energy

4. A Study of Environments

Food chains and food webs

109. (a) (i) sun (light)
         (ii) starch
         (iii) sycamore (this is a green plant)
         (iv) owl
         (v) syc. leaves → worm → mole → owl
                                     ↘ badger
         (vi) The number of moles will reduce: less food is available so some will starve.

109. (b) (i) $\frac{950}{10\,000} \times \frac{100}{1} = 9.5\%$
     (ii) Any two from:
         · heat
         · movement
         · waste produced
         · parts not eaten

110. 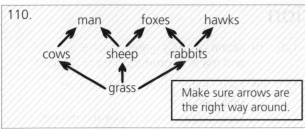 Make sure arrows are the right way around.	112. variety of organisms present, many links
	113. (a)

Year	Mass of crops lost (kg/ha)
1949	600
1955	150
1960	120

(b) (i) Pesticides on crops. Small mammals eat the crops. Pesticides get into the small mammals. Kestrels eat many small mammals and pesticides build up in their bodies.
(ii) The number of one kind (species) of animal or plant in a place. |
| 111. (a) 1 = bubbles of gas/oxygen
2 = test tube
3 = pond weed/plant
4 = water
5 = Plasticene
(b) Line graph:
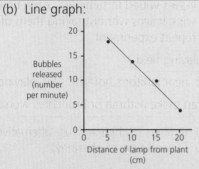
(c) The closer the lamp, the more bubbles *or* the further away the lamp, the less bubbles.
(d) *Any one from*: temperature of the water, lamp type, volume of water, how well she timed the experiment, how accurately she counted the bubbles, how accurately she measured the distance of the lamp. | 114. (a) Liwi
(b) The Ou has banded markings on head and its diet includes fruit.
(c) Grosbeak Finch |
| | 115. (a) B
(b) Potatoes. More energy gained from shorter food chain. Less energy lost. |
| | 116. (a) D
(b) decomposers
(c) consumers |

Interdependence and populations

117. *Any three from*: temperature, light intensity, rainfall, soil pH, humidity	119. (a) Year 2
(b) Year 3. Low rainfall, less heather growth, less food for grouse so fewer grouse.
118. (a) (i) Averages: Area 1 = 11, Area 2 = 31
(ii) light intensity
(iii) The more light, the more daisy plants. (Daisy plants only grow well in bright light.)
(b) *Any one from*: competition for space, competition for water, temperature, rainfall, soil pH, and humidity	120. Group B growing better. Less overcrowded so more light and water for each plant.

Production and recycling of household waste

121. (a) (i) plastic = 50%, paper = 25%, metal = 10%, glass = 5%, other = 10%.
(ii) *Any one from*: food waste, old clothes/rags, ashes
(b) (i) 'Recycled' means used again.
(ii) Recycling metal saves energy, resources, money, helps protect the environment.
(c) 70% more	121. (d) saves trees, plus advantages given in (b) (ii)
(e) (i) less
(ii) More plastic and paper now because more packaging; plastics not much in use 50 years ago; fewer magazines and newspapers 50 years ago.
(f) $\frac{2}{5} \times 100 = 40\%$ was paper.

Pollution

122.

Part of the environment	Example of a pollutant
land	Any one from: household rubbish industrial rubbish excess fertilisers excess pesticides
sea or water	sewage
air	Any one from: smoke soot sulphur dioxide carbon dioxide carbon monoxide oxides of nitrogen

123. *Any one from:* sulphur dioxide, carbon monoxide, carbon dioxide, oxides of nitrogen

124. (a) C D B E A

    (b) *Any two of:*
- same number of seedlings
- same type of seedlings
- same age of seedlings
- same temperature of air
- same size of dish
- same volume of cotton wool
- same light intensity
- same total volume of liquid added

125. (a) carbon dioxide or methane

    (b) *Any one from:* global warming, change in weather patterns, flooding of low-lying land, melting icecaps

126. (a) ozone layer

    (b) action of CFCs (gases in some aerosols and made in producing some plastics)

127. (a) Near janitor's house had most air pollution.
Explanation: this leaf was the dirtiest.

    (b) *Any two of:*
- same size of tissue
- leaves the same size
- same type of leaf
- leaves gathered from same height
- leaves wiped in same way each time
- wipe leaves without taking them off tree
- repeat experiment

    (c) playing field

    (d) (i) near janitor's house   (ii) playing field

    (e) can make asthma or bronchitis worse

    (f) (i) fit filters to chimneys; use alternative fuels
       (ii) fit scrubbers to chimneys

128. (a) between B and C

    (b) (i) high
       (ii) about 20 (Any figure between 9 and 23 is acceptable.)

    (c) (i) The change is from 23 to 4. This means there are 19 less per m^3.
       (ii) At B oxygen high, so many invertebrates can survive; at C oxygen low, so few survive.

    (d) (i) Plants need light to grow. Light does not get through cloudy water, so few plants can grow.
       (ii) A and B

Human needs and conservation

129. food, water, shelter, air and warmth

130. food and water

131. (a) loss of animals' food and places to live

    (b) Difference means 'take away' so
24 − 9 = 15% more land covered in desert

    (c) $8000\ km^2 \times 54\% = 8000 \times \dfrac{54}{100}$
= 4320 km^2 destroyed

132. Conservation is the way of meeting humans' basic needs without spoiling the environment.

133. $60\,000 \times 96\% = 60\,000 \times \dfrac{96}{100} = 57\,600$
57 600 is the number they are reduced by. So, 60 000 − 57 600 = 2400 are left in the wild.

134. (a) 3 + 2 + 2 + 1 = 8.
Divide by 4 for average = 2 per km^2

    (b) Total area = 300 km^2
Average of 2 per km^2 = 300 × 2
                               = 600 Gorillas

    (c) There are none left in the world (they have all died out).

    (d) *Any two from:*
- set up captive breeding programmes, then release the Gorillas back into the wild
- make the species protected by law
- set up nature reserves, national parks or game reserves so that the place where they live is protected

Miscellaneous materials questions

74. Here is a chart showing the components of one particular grade of concrete (before mixing with water).

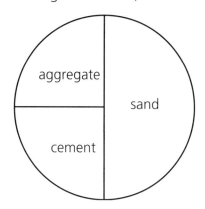

   (a) What percentage of the concrete is made up of sand?

   (b) If 3 kg of cement is used, how much sand should be used?

   (c) If 3 kg of cement is used, what would be the total weight of the concrete (before the water is added)?

75. List three things that are often flameproofed by the manufacturers.

76. Carbon monoxide is a poisonous gas given off when many things burn. What effect does carbon monoxide have on the human body that can cause brain damage or even death?

77. Jack and Jill are having a competition to see who can stack the most 50p coins on a sweetie tube. Jack lays the tube on its side while Jill stands it up on its end.

   (a) Who do you think will win the competition?

   (b) Explain your answer.

See pages 15 to 24 of Leckie & Leckie's *Standard Grade Science Revision Notes*

3. Energy and its Uses

Energy in the home

78. The electricity meter in a house gave the following readings over a three-month period:

   1st reading 2 6 4 0 6
   2nd reading 2 9 6 1 3

   Each unit of electricity costs the user 8 pence. What would the electricity bill be for this three-month period?

79. Copy and complete the table below to show the cost of using different electrical appliances in the home. The missing entries have been replaced by the letters (a) to (i).

   Here is how to calculate (a):

   100 W bulb = 0·1 kW
   energy used (in kWh) = power rating (in kW) × time of use (in hours)
   = 0·1 × 10 = 1·0 kWh
   total cost = 1·0 × 8 p = 8 p

   Now calculate the other missing entries.

Appliance	Time of use (hours)	Energy used (kWh)	Cost per kWh	Total cost
100 W bulb	10	1·0	8 p	(a)
2·5 kW fire	(b)	(c)	8 p	80 p
1·0 kW iron	(d)	2	8 p	(e)
(f) fan heater	6	(g)	8 p	96 p
200 W freezer	100	(h)	8 p	(i)

80. (a) What is the purpose of a thermostat?
   (b) List three appliances or systems in the home that contain thermostats.
   (c) Explain fully how a 'bimetallic strip' thermostat works.

81. The diagram below shows the areas through which heat is lost from the home.

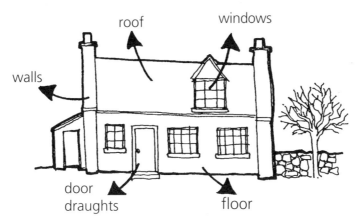

(a) Give one way heat loss may be reduced from each of the following areas of the house:
   (i) roof
   (ii) windows
   (iii) floor
   (iv) walls
   (v) door

(b) Energy is lost from homes by conduction, convection and radiation. Which one is the main method of heat loss through draughty doorways?

82. Study the chart below and then answer the questions.

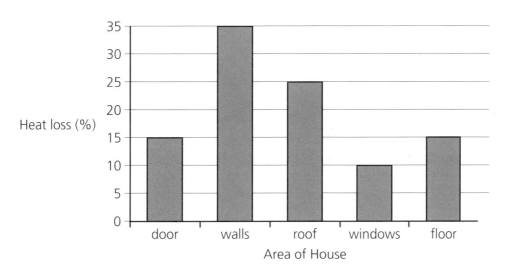

(a) Which area of the house has the highest percentage heat loss?

(b) What is the percentage heat loss through the windows?

(c) If you were the owner of this house and you could afford to buy double glazing or loft insulation (but not both), which would you choose? Explain your answer.

Electrical safety

83. 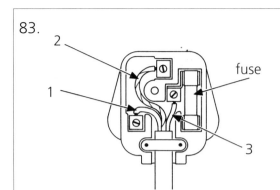 Copy and complete the following table.

Wire	Name	Colour
1	Neutral	
2		
3		

84. Copy and complete the following passage using the wordbank below:

The Earth wire is a _____ device. It is connected to the outer casing of _____ appliances. If a _____ occurs and the outer casing becomes _____, the _____ wire will carry a large _____ to ground and cause the _____ to melt. The appliance is now _____ and therefore _____.

Wordbank	off, fault, safety, metal, current, fuse, live, earth, safe

Warning! Electricity can kill.

85. Hamish has been given the task of choosing the correct fuse for some appliances in his house. He has 3 amp and 13 amp fuses available. Which value of fuse should Hamish choose for each of the appliances listed below?

(a) 2000 watt kettle

(b) 100 watt lamp

(c) 1000 watt television

(d) 450 watt radio

(e) 3 kilowatt electric fire

(f) 1·5 kilowatt drill

86. Formula: $P = I \times V$

    where P = Power rating (watts)
            I = Current (amps)
            V = Voltage (volts)

    Use the above formula to calculate the values of (a), (b), (c) and (d) in the table below.

Power rating (watts)	Current (amps)	Voltage (volts)
2400	(a)	240
(b)	2·5	240
(c)	5	240
816	(d)	240

87. Calum noticed that the electric iron he was using to press his kilt had a label with 1200 W marked on it. Which one of the following is true?

    A. 1200 W is the current rating
    B. 1200 W is the voltage rating
    C. 1200 W is the power rating
    D. 1200 W is the fuse rating

88. Cables connecting electrical appliances to the mains supply can overheat and even catch fire if the current through them is too high. Explain how the fuse in the plug helps to prevent the danger of overheating cables and damage to electrical appliances. Use the list of keywords to help.

Keywords	fuse, wire, current, melt, safety device, thin

89. The fuse in a mains plug is always connected to the Live wire.
    The switch in a mains socket is also always connected to the Live wire.
    Explain why these rules must be obeyed.

Fossil fuels

90. Explain what is meant by:

    (a) renewable energy sources

    (b) non-renewable energy sources.

91. List three renewable energy sources and three non-renewable energy sources.

92. Describe how coal was formed.

93. The formation of oil is similar to that of coal. State the main difference between the formation of oil and the formation of coal.

94. Below is a diagram of one of the ways in which oil and gas are trapped with water underground. Identify the three layers labelled a, b and c.

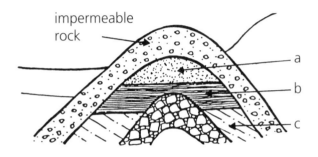

95. Drilling of test holes is one method of detecting oil. Describe the other three methods listed below:

  (a) seismic survey   (b) aerial survey   (c) geological survey.

96. The chart below shows the relative consumption of different fossil fuels in the fictional town of East Glenington. This includes industrial, domestic and all transport uses.

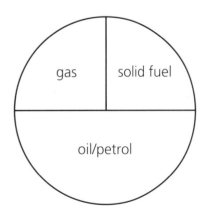

(a) What percentage of the fossil fuels used is gas?

(b) The total fossil fuel consumption in East Glenington is 800 gigajoules in one year. What would the consumption (in gigajoules) have been of:
  (i) oil/petrol
  (ii) gas
  (iii) solid fuel?

97. Copy and complete the following passage using the wordbank below.

The _____ oil extracted from the ground has to be _____ , i.e. split into useful parts in a _____ tower. The parts into which the oil is split are called _____ . This process depends upon the different parts having different _____ _____ . The temperature at the bottom of the tower is much _____ and therefore substances with _____ boiling points are taken off there. Substances from the bottom of the tower are _____ coloured whereas those substances from higher up the tower (with _____ boiling points) are _____ coloured.

| Wordbank | fractions, light, refined, dark, fractionating, higher, lower, crude, boiling points, high |

98. Some of the gases produced by the burning of fossil fuels can cause serious pollution problems. The gases may damage the environment and/or the health of the population.
   (a) (i) Which gas is the major cause of 'acid rain'?
       (ii) What are the main effects of acid rain on the environment?
   (b) (i) Which gas is the major contributor to the 'greenhouse effect'?
       (ii) In what way does this affect the entire planet?

99. Copy and complete the table below showing some of the products obtained from crude oil. Give one use for each product and give its point of extraction from the tower.

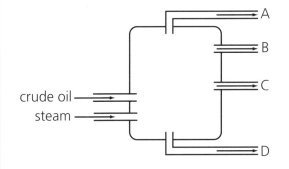

Product	Use	Extraction point (A, B, C, or D)
petrol		
bitumen		
naphtha		
petroleum gases		
diesel		
paraffin		
wax		

100. Copy and complete the following representation of the energy conversions that take place in a coal-fired power station. Use the list of energy forms provided.

_____ energy → _____ energy → _____ energy → Electrical energy.

| **Energy Forms** | Heat, Movement (Kinetic), Chemical |

101. Identify the labels in this simplified diagram of a coal-fired power station.

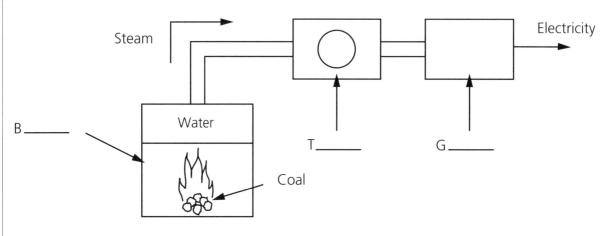

102. This is part of the index of a book about energy.

```
Alternative                          Nuclear
    solar ................. 214          hazards ............. 185
    waves ................ 221          safety ............... 194
    wind ................. 218      Oil
    others ............... 223          formation ........... 80
Coal                                     extraction .......... 85
    formation ............ 38           refining ............ 101
    extraction ........... 45           uses ................ 120
    uses ................. 64       Pollution ............... 205
```

(a) Which page would you look up to find out about the use of pig manure as an energy source?

(b) Which page would you look up to find out how petrol is obtained from crude oil?

(c) Which two pages would be the best to look up to find out about possible harmful effects on humans caused by the energy industries?

103. Match each type of fire (1 – 5) to the extinguisher (A, B or C) that should be used to put each fire out safely.

Type of fire
1. forest fire
2. chip pan fire
3. television on fire
4. petrol tanker fire
5. electric oven on fire

Extinguisher
A. fire blanket
B. water
C. powder or carbon dioxide

Nuclear energy

104. Nuclear power stations produce harmful waste. The level of radioactivity of this waste reduces very slowly, as shown in the table below.

Time (years)	Radioactivity (counts per min.)
0	40 000
100	33 000
200	26 000
300	20 000
400	16 000
500	13 000
600	10 000
700	8000
800	6500
900	5000
1000	3700

(a) From this table construct a line graph (on graph paper) to show how the radioactivity falls with time.

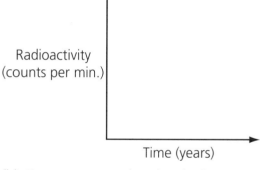

(b) From your graph, what is the radioactivity after 160 years?

(c) (i) What does the term 'half-life' mean?
    (ii) What is the half-life of the radioactive waste in this question?

105. What form of energy is produced in the reactor of a nuclear power station? Choose one of the options below:

   A. Chemical energy

   B. Kinetic (movement) energy

   C. Heat energy

   D. Electrical energy

Renewable energy

106. The energy needed to heat up any substance is given by:

   $E = m \times c \times (T_2 - T_1)$ joules

   where
   m = mass of substance (kg)
   c = a constant (different for each different substance)
   T_2 = final temperature (°C)
   T_1 = starting temperature (°C)

   Calculate the energy needed to heat up 5 kg of water from 20°C to 70°C.
   c (of water) = 4200 J/kg °C

107. The power output from a small wind-powered generator was recorded for varying wind speeds. The results are shown below.

Wind speed (mph)	Power output (watts)
0	0
5	100
10	180
15	260
20	320
30	350
40	350
50	350

   (a) Present these results as a line graph.

   (b) What conclusions can be drawn?

108. What name is given to the energy source that involves using the heat stored in rocks deep underground?

4. A Study of Environments

Food chains and food webs

109. Here is a food chain.

sycamore leaves → earthworm → mole → owl

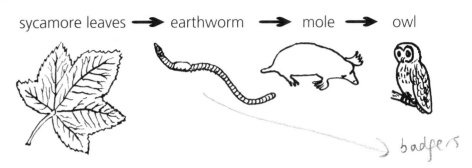

→ badgers

(a) (i) What provides the energy for the sycamore leaves? Sun
(ii) What food is stored in the sycamore leaves? starch
(iii) Which organism is the producer? sycamore tree
(iv) Which organism is the predator of the mole? owl
(v) Earthworms are also eaten by badgers. Copy the food chain and add an extra link to show this feeding relationship.
(vi) British earthworms are being killed by an invasion of New Zealand flatworms. What effect will this have on the number of moles? ↓

(b) The arrows in a food chain indicate that energy passes from one organism to another. A mole takes in 10 000 kJ of energy by eating earthworms. The owl only gains 950 kJ of energy by eating one mole.
950/10,000 ×100 =70% 9·5%
(i) What percentage of the energy taken in by the mole is passed to the owl?
(ii) Give two ways that energy is lost from the food chain at this stage. heat waste movement

110. Grass is eaten by cows, rabbits and sheep.
Rabbits are eaten by foxes and hawks.
Sheep and cows are eaten by man.
Foxes will also eat young or injured sheep.

Use the information above to draw a food web.
The web will show the plant, all the animals and their feeding relationships.

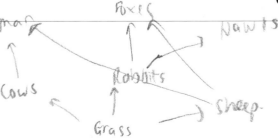

111. All green plants use light energy to make food. The plants also give out oxygen which animals need to breathe.

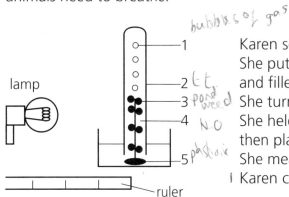

Karen set up an experiment.
She put a piece of pond weed inside a test tube and filled the test tube with water.
She turned the test tube upside down over a dish.
She held the pond weed in place with Plasticene, then placed a lamp 20 cm away from the plant.
She measured the distance with a ruler.
Karen could see bubbles of gas.

Labels (handwritten): 1 – bubbles of gas; 2 – tt; 3 – pond weed; 4 – H₂O; 5 – plasticine

(a) Copy the above diagram and use the information to add labels to the numbered guidelines.

(b) Karen counted the number of bubbles given off by the pond weed in one minute. She moved the lamp closer so that it was 15 cm away from the plant and counted the number of bubbles again. She then repeated this at distances of 10 cm and 5 cm.

Results:

Distance of lamp from plant (cm)	Bubbles released (number per minute)
5	18
10	14
15	10
20	4

Use graph paper to produce a line graph of the above results.

(c) What conclusion could Karen draw about the distance of the lamp from the plant and the number of bubbles produced? ↓ dist → ↑ no. of bubbles

(d) Experiments have to be fair. So, each time Karen moved the lamp, she left the experiment to settle for a few minutes before counting the bubbles.
She repeated the experiment and worked out averages.
She used the same piece of pond weed each time.
Give one other factor which might have affected the fairness of the experiment.
temp.

112. The natural food web in a well-established woodland is very stable. What makes a food web stable? lots of links

113. Modern farming methods include the use of pesticides. The introduction of pesticides greatly reduces the mass of crops lost to pests. Rice production in Japan in 1949 involved a loss of 600 kg/ha. By 1955 pesticides were in use and the loss was 150 kg/ha. There was a further improvement to 120 kg/ha by 1960.

   (a) Present the above information about loss of crops in a table with two suitable headings.

   (b) Pesticides are popular with farmers for improving crop yield. Pesticides are less popular with people concerned with wildlife. Even small amounts of pesticide sprayed on crops can cause a decrease in the population of kestrels. Kestrels do not eat crops, they kill and eat small mammals such as mice and voles.
   (i) Explain how the kestrels become affected by pesticides. *pst > crops mice eat crops*
   (ii) What is meant by the term 'population'? *voles eat m*

   No. of orgs in 1 place

114.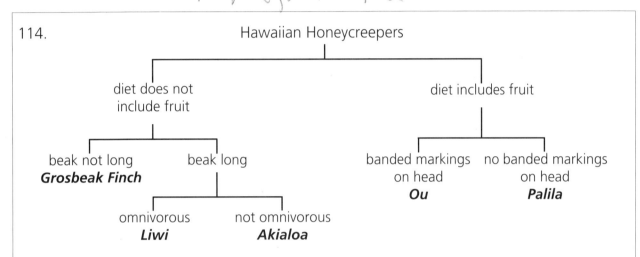

   Hawaiian Honeycreepers are finch-like birds.
   There are different species of these birds shown in the key above.

   (a) Which species does not eat fruit, has a long beak and is omnivorous? *Liwi*
   (b) Describe the **Ou** using features shown in the key. *eats fruit banded m.*
   (c) A sixth species of Honeycreeper has a short beak, has banded markings on its head and does not eat fruit. It is closely related to one species named in the key. Which one? *Grosbeak Finch*

115. A. potato ➔ pig ➔ man
   B. potato ➔ man

   (a) Two food chains are shown above. Which food chain will have the least loss of energy overall? *B*

   (b) In parts of South America there is the problem of too many people and a shortage of food. Farmers in South America could grow potatoes or they could farm pigs. Which should they produce? Potatoes or pigs? Explain your answer. *potatoes*

116. Waste is produced in a natural environment such as a hillside covered with trees. The waste is constantly recycled.

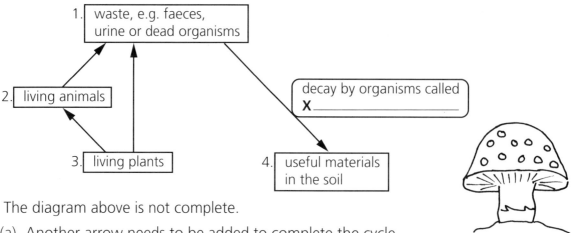

The diagram above is not complete.

(a) Another arrow needs to be added to complete the cycle. Where should this arrow be drawn? Select the correct answer.

A. from box 1 to box 4
B. from box 2 to box 4
C. from box 4 to box 2
D. from box 4 to box 3

(b) What word should be added at **X**?

(c) The organisms which cause decay use the waste as their food. Are these organisms producers or consumers?

Interdependence and populations

117. Cactus plants do not grow well in Scottish gardens. Most will die in the winter. Give three environmental factors which affect the growth of cactus plants.

118. The members of a class carried out a survey of the number of daisy plants in their school playing field. Four groups of pupils counted the number of daisy plants. They looked at two different areas and counted the plants in 1 metre squares.

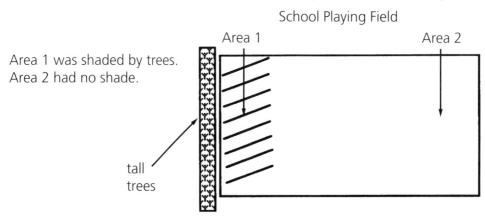

Area 1 was shaded by trees.
Area 2 had no shade.

118. (cont.)

    Results

Survey area	Number of daisy plants per 1 m square				Average
	Group 1	Group 2	Group 3	Group 4	
1 (shaded)	7	13	8	16	?
2 (no shade)	29	32	35	28	?

    (a) (i) Calculate the averages for area 1 and area 2.
    (ii) What environmental factor was most likely to be affecting the growth of the daisy plants?
    (iii) What conclusion could the class reach about this environmental factor and daisy plants?

    (b) The number of daisy plants may also be affected by other factors such as the number of animals present which eat them. Give one other factor which might limit the size of the daisy population in any area.

119. The number of grouse living on Scottish moorland varies from year to year depending on their food supply. Grouse eat heather shoots. The wetter the weather, the more the heather plants grow.

    A Scottish gamekeeper has the following information on record.

Year of survey	Summer weather conditions (3 months)	
	Rainfall	Average daytime temperature
1	high	cool
2	very high	warm
3	low	very warm
4	high	cool

    (a) The gamekeeper had noted that the heather growth was very good one summer. Which year of the survey was this most likely to be?

    (b) In which year of the survey would the grouse numbers be low? Explain your answer.

120. A family moved into a new house. The garden had no plants in it. In the spring, the mother decided to put in some plants. She bought twenty marigold plants and put them in two different parts of the front garden.

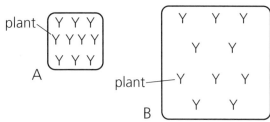

By the summer, one group of plants was growing better than the other.
Which group (A or B) is likely to be the one growing better?
Explain your answer.

Production and recycling of household waste

121. The waste produced by a household was collected and measured for one week. The results were used to draw a pie chart.

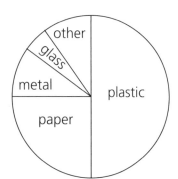

Type of waste	Content (%)
plastic	
paper	
metal	
glass	
other	

(a) (i) Copy and complete the table by using information from the pie chart.
   (ii) Name one type of waste which might be in the 'other' group.

(b) (i) The metal in the waste can be recycled. What does recycled mean?
   (ii) Why is it good for the environment to recycle as much metal as possible?

(c) About 75% of household waste could be recycled. Most households only recycle about 5%.
    What percentage more could be recycled?

(d) Paper is made from wood. What advantage is there in using recycled paper?

(e) Fifty years ago, the waste from a household would have been quite different. There would have been a lot of ashes in the rubbish bin because most houses had coal fires. Now, most houses do not have coal fires. The amount of plastic and paper in the bin is now different too.
   (i) Look at the amounts of paper and plastic above. Would there have been more or less of these wastes in a bin fifty years ago?
   (ii) Why is there a different amount of paper and plastic in the waste now?

(f) The weight of rubbish produced in one week from a different household was 5 kg.
    The weight of paper in this rubbish was 2 kg.
    What percentage of this rubbish was paper?

Pollution

122. Pollution can affect three main parts of the environment. Copy and complete the table.

Part of the environment	Example of a pollutant
land	
	sewage
air	

123. Pollutants are substances which result in pollution. Car exhaust fumes contain a number of different pollutants, such as lead from some cars. Name one other pollutant found in car exhaust fumes.

124. Elizabeth set up an experiment to test the effect of acid rain on the growth of seedlings. The steps are in the wrong order.

   A. count how many seedlings are still growing
   B. add a different volume of acid to each dish
   C. set up five dishes of seedlings
   D. measure out five different volumes of weak acid
   E. leave the seedlings for two days

   (a) List the steps in the correct order. Start with step C.

   (b) One of the dishes set up for step C looked like this:

   Elizabeth then set up the other four dishes.
   State two things she would have to keep the same to make the experiment fair.

125. The greenhouse effect may produce global warming and cause problems across the world.

   (a) Name one gas which produces the greenhouse effect.
   (b) Give one result of the greenhouse effect.

126. There is a layer of gas high in the atmosphere which filters out harmful U.V. light rays. Damage to this layer allows the U.V. rays through.

   (a) What name is given to this layer of gas?

   (b) Give one way this layer of gas can be damaged.

127. Paul did an experiment to measure air pollution. He gathered 4 leaves from trees in different areas around the school.

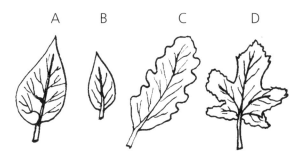

He wiped each leaf once with a piece of white tissue.
He then compared the colour of the tissues.

Leaf	Tree site	Tissue colour
A	playing field	light grey
B	near janitor's house	almost black
C	school gates	dark grey
D	behind PE block	dark grey

   (a) Which area had most air pollution? Explain your answer.

   (b) Give two ways that the experiment method could be improved.

   (c) Paul thought that the soot might be coming from the exhausts of passing traffic. If this is true, which site is most likely to be far away from the traffic?

   (d) Lichens are simple plants which are found growing on tree trunks and walls. They are sensitive to the amount of sulphur dioxide pollution in the air. The more sulphur dioxide in the air, the fewer lichens can survive. If Paul also counted the number of lichens on the tree trunks in the sites of his survey, where would he find
   (i) least lichens?
   (ii) most lichens?

   (e) Air pollution can affect people's health.
   Name one way air pollution can damage health.

   (f) How could factories
   (i) reduce the amount of soot in chimney smoke?
   (ii) reduce the amount of sulphur dioxide in chimney smoke?

128. Five samples of river water were taken at points shown in the diagram below.

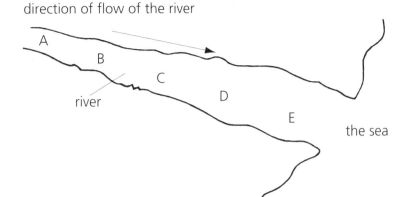

Results

Sample point	A	B	C	D	E
Oxygen concentration	high	high	low	medium	high
Bacteria count	low	low	?	medium	low
Invertebrate count (number per m³)	21	23	4	9	?
Cloudiness of water (scale: 0 = clear; 5 = cloudy)	0	0	5	3	1

(a) Between which points has the organic pollution level increased?

(b) Some entries have been missed out of the table.
   (i) What word would you put in for the bacteria count at C?
   (ii) Suggest a figure for the invertebrate count at E.

(c) (i) The count of invertebrates changes between points B and C. What is the change in the number of invertebrates?
   (ii) Bacteria use up oxygen in the water. The more bacteria in the water, the less oxygen there is. Use this information to explain the change in the count of invertebrates between points B and C.

(d) Where sewage levels are high, the water is cloudy.
   Where sewage levels are high, there are not many water plants growing.
   (i) Explain why water plants will not grow well where sewage levels are high.
   (ii) At which two sample points would you expect the most plants to be growing?

Human needs and conservation

129. Name the five basic needs of human beings.

130. A family sets off to live in a sailing boat for a year.
The boat has heaters in the rooms inside to give them shelter and warmth. There are windows they can open and they can go up on deck. What will they need to take with them to meet their other basic needs?

131. The planet Earth is changing.

    (a) Some humans living in parts of South America are changing the environment. They are clearing away natural forests to plough the land for crops.
    Although crops are needed for food, this is causing harm.
    How can clearing natural forests harm animals?

    (b) About 70 years ago, deserts covered 9% of the planet. Deserts now cover over 24% of the planet's surface. Calculate the difference in percentage of land covered in deserts.

    (c) Wetlands are disappearing from all around the world. In the southern United States, approximately 8000 km^2 was originally wetland. About 54% of this has now been destroyed. Calculate the area of wetland that has been destroyed.

132. State the meaning of the term 'conservation'.

133. Twenty years ago there were 60 000 Black Rhino in the wild. The numbers have now reduced by 96%. How many Black Rhinos are left in the wild?

134. Mountain Gorillas live in only a few parts of Africa.
The total area in which they are found is approximately 300 km^2.
Counts of the numbers of Mountain Gorillas in different sites gave the following results:

Site	Number per km^2
Uganda (site 1)	3
Uganda (site 2)	2
Zaire	2
Rwanda	1

    (a) What is the average number of Mountain Gorillas per km^2?
    (b) Calculate approximately how many Gorillas there are in the total area.
    (c) If nothing is done, Gorillas will become extinct. What does 'extinct' mean?
    (d) Describe two ways that conservation workers could try to stop Gorillas from becoming extinct.

See pages 43 and 44 of Leckie & Leckie's *Standard Grade Science Revision Notes*